I0390539

Interview

The Ultimate Guide to Crushing Every Interview Question to Land Your Dream Job

David Barron

Golden Road Publishing

Table of Contents

Table of Contents 3

Introduction 4

Chapter 1: Change the Way You Think About Interviews 7

Chapter 2: Get an Interview 19

Chapter 3: Receive an Interview Invitation like a True Professional 34

Chapter 4: The Planning and Preparation Phase 45

Chapter 5: What To Do While Waiting 66

Chapter 6: Making a Brilliant First Impression 74

Chapter 7: Be a Dynamic Listener and a Smart Speaker 84

Chapter 8: The Ten Most Important Interview Questions and How to Answer Them 102

Final Thoughts 121

References 124

About the Author 126

Introduction

An interviewer's question may take all shapes and forms. However, all these enquiries merely boil down to the ultimate question: *WHY SHOULD WE HIRE YOU?* This simple question is not something that can be answered with a few sentences, and is not a question that you should take lightly. This is, instead, answered by everything that you say and do from the time you greet your interviewer and the interview comes to an end, all the way up to what goes on after the interview in the post-interview stage. This question is answered by the promptness in which you show up at the office, by how you choose to fix your hair, and even by the frequency to which you mirror your interviewer's speech and body language.

In a manner of speaking, a job interview is your one great opportunity to sell yourself to a potential employer in a fixed period of time. Everything that you say or do during an interview is a chance to show your future employer that you're the right person for the job. Even when you're answering questions about your hobbies or the kind of books you like to read, the interviewer is constantly assessing whether you're someone worth hiring.

In order to make a sale, you first have to know what that person *needs* so that you may show and convince him that what you're selling is fully qualified to cater to those needs. For this reason, conducting research about the company, the job, and the employer beforehand is an essential move prior to showing up at any interview, regardless of whether you're applying for a part-time job or for an executive position at a Fortune 500 company. If you look at it this way, you'll understand that the success of a job interview lies not only in the interview itself, but also in the efforts you expend before the actual interview occurs. This is why this book explores all phases and aspects of the job interview, from the preparation period to the follow-up stage. This guide takes you into a systematic journey from securing a job interview to closing the deal like a true professional.

One common mistake that interviewees do is to memorize pre-set questions and answers. They neglect this one important fact: Interviewers are ultimately impressed not with the interviewees who supply the "best" answers, but rather with the individuals who are able to answer their questions the best. Thus, preparing for an interview is about developing your skill to respond to any kind of question that your interviewer may throw right off the bat. While this book may include only ten interview questions, you'll find that these questions are the only ones that actually matter. If you can answer these, then you can answer them any variation.

A job interview is synonymous to a door that will either open up and usher you into a fulfilling career or slam itself shut in your face. This metaphorical door goes two ways. An interview is not just a tool for a prospective employer to assess whether you are the right person for the job. It is also your way to gauge whether the job, the employer, and/or the company is right for you.

The aim of this book is plain and simple: To provide a factual, well-researched guide, which will aid entry-level and experienced professionals in succeeding in an interview. This way, you can get the job that you've always wanted!

Chapter 1: Change the Way You Think About Interviews

What is an interview?

Of course you know what an interview is. After all, interviews are a fact of modern professional life. In a one-to-one meeting, the interviewer asks you a bunch of questions to evaluate whether or not you're the right person for the job. But what is an interview, really? What is its ultimate purpose?

So far, the greatest expense of companies and employers is their workforce. Employees' salaries constitute over 70% of a business's total expenses. For this reason, mistakes in recruitment can cost companies a great deal of money and time. For instance, disgruntled employees lead to poor productivity, which cause them to become liabilities to the business instead of assets. Similarly, conflicts within the workplace end up destabilizing the entire team and will inevitably end up threatening the function of the whole organization. This is why employers and companies take extra steps (such as preliminary interviews before the final interview) in ensuring that they end up selecting the right candidates for the job. As far as employers are concerned, the "right candidate" refers to the person who will be able to contribute most to the interests of the company.

An interview, in the simplest sense, is a discussion between two (or more) individuals. Companies, employers, and organizations use interviewing as a tool to assist them in selecting the best applicants. The term "best" is entirely flexible. While one candidate may have more experience or a broader range of skills compared to another, the latter may be the one who *best* fits the company's or the organization's vision.

Despite a comparatively inferior academic background, an applicant may be chosen above others simply because of other qualities (such as social skills, ability to cooperate with co-workers, etc.), which the employer deems more important. In other words, you must keep in mind that in job interviews, employers aren't looking for people who are the best in their fields. Rather, they are looking for people who are the *best fit for their specific company's/business's goals.*

This is the part where one of the greatest myths about interviews will be debunked:

The interviewer is interested in you.

He's not. Just as you're not really interested in your interviewer. What you're interested in is yourself and your well-being: How to get the job that you want, how to succeed in your chosen career, how to increase your compensation, etc. Likewise, what your employer cares about is his business. When he's interviewing you, he's actually thinking about how you (your skills, your experience, your personality, etc.) will help his business improve. From this fact, you will learn one of the greatest lessons that you need to know about conducting yourself in interviews:

Even while you're selling yourself, you need to ultimately make the whole interview about the company/business.

For instance, you don't tell your future employer that you have excellent problem-solving skills just so you could paint a pretty picture of yourself. You tell your employer this because you know that his company *needs* and *will benefit* from someone who has excellent problem-solving skills.

As far as your employer is concerned, the only time you matter is as long as you are able to contribute something to the good of the business.

So, how do you make yourself matter to your future employer?

You start off by dropping your own needs and wants and by focusing on these questions:

What does my potential employer need?

What does he want?

What are the problems that concern him?

How can I help his business/company become better/more profitable?

Let's say your employer asks you: "Why are you applying for this job?"

The most honest answer to that would be: "For the salary."

But of course, to answer in this way would most likely lead to zero job offers. That's because the employer doesn't want to hear about how you're present in this job interview to solve *your* problems. What he wants to hear is how you're in this job interview to provide solutions to *his* problems.

Of course, to know exactly what your potential employer needs, you have to conduct research prior to the interview. The things you need to investigate are:

The Industry (in general)

> *What are the current trends?* Make sure that you are up-to-date with the latest discoveries and innovations in the industry. Familiarize yourself with the movers and shakers in the field. This will show how well-informed and passionate you are about your profession.
>
> Then, ask yourself this: *Do I possess any skills or experiences that will show the employer that I am competent in the field?*
>
> No business owner wants his company to be left behind. Thus, employers appreciate

individuals who are open to the idea of continuous learning. In other words, they want people who can keep up.

The Company

Find out as much as you can about the company/organization that you're applying for. What are its methods of producing revenue? What is the company's vision and mission? Read up about the company's history.

This will show that you really are interested in being a part of the company. More than that though, this will enable you to determine how you're going to prove to the employer that you're someone who can carry out the company's goals.

Not all employers know exactly what they want or need. By studying their company's methods and current performance, you can make it your job to *show* your potential employer what he/she needs.

The Interviewer

This won't be too much of a challenge especially if the person is of notable standing in the field. Like it or not, interviews are rarely unbiased. After all, you *are* being interviewed by a human being. It *is* possible for you to rub an interviewer the wrong way with your personality, your body language, or your looks. It *is* possible for you to chance upon an interviewer on a bad day. For this reason, it is important to know how to provide the best first impression. More of this will be discussed later.

From here, you'll be able to gather this essential lesson:

You need to stop thinking about interviews in terms of providing correct answers all the time. Interviews are as much about creating rapport and trust as they are about answering questions intelligently.

Are you as good as you claim yourself to be?

There is only one reason why an employer will invite you for an interview: He wants to find out more about you. This means he wants to find out more about what you can do for his business/company. This way, he can ascertain whether you are the best person for the job.

One common myth that people still believe is that they are called in for interviews so the employers can test if they will crack under pressure or to determine how they will respond to trick questions. You need to understand that interviewers, especially those ranked high in the chain of command, have neither the time nor the leisure to "torture" their applicants. Like you, they are expending precious time and energy just to conduct the interview. Hiring the right person is *that* important to them.

If you've been invited for a job interview, then chances are, your CV has captured your potential employer's interest at the very least. Now, he wants to verify if his initial impression about you was accurate. In other words, he wants to see if you're as good in person as you are on paper. He also wants to know how you will deal with future situations that are most likely to pop up in your target job. So far, everything that you've said and done up to this point has been effective. Now, all that's left for you to do is to prove that you are, in fact, the person that you had painted yourself to be. This means that before showing up at the interview, it is essential that you re-read all the things that you've put in your CV. Some of the questions that the interviewer will ask you will be based on what you've stated in your resume.

What if you're not as good as you claim to be?

Whether or not you'll get the job is based on how well you satisfy the interviewer on these three areas:

- Job qualifications and skills (*What do you know? What can you do?*)

- Job experience (*Where have you been and what have you done?*)

- Personality (*Who are you? How will you conduct yourself among co-workers, clients, etc. once you're hired?*)

Of all these traits, employers find the third one to be the most important. After all, it's easy enough to educate and train a person... but to change someone's personality? That's an entirely different story. For this reason, even when an applicant ends up falling short of his advertised skills, he can still manage to persuade interviewers that he is the perfect person for the position.

In one study, two psychologists performed a thorough analysis on large data sets of job interview information in order to determine which personality attributes hiring companies seek. Sackett and Walmsley (2014) were able to determine that out of several necessary qualities of applicants, employers value personality traits such as dependability, perseverance, and orderliness most of all. Meanwhile, the research revealed that tolerance, cooperation, and flexibility are the second most sought-after traits which employers wish to see more of in applicants.

Remember:

In an ideal universe, the best man or woman for the job will definitely get the part. In the real world, however, the person who wins the position is the one who is able to perform best *during the interview*. Thus, when you apply for a position alongside someone whom you think is more qualified, don't back out. If you expend enough effort in preparing for the job interview, it's possible that the interviewer will regard you as a more suitable candidate than your highly qualified, but inadequately prepared, rival.

Likewise, if you believe that you are the one most suited for the position and if you believe that the company will be lucky to have you, then don't use this as a justification to slack off. The fact that you're *this* close to getting your dream job should provide you with even more reason to prepare for the interview. You need to act as if you're head-to-head against powerful competitors because you are. Yes, you may be the perfect man or woman for the job. But the question is: Do you know how to communicate this fact in a language that your potential employer will appreciate and understand?

Chapter 2: Get an Interview

In order to succeed in an interview, you first need to land one. So how, in the sea of desperate hopefuls, will you make yourself stand out as a suitable candidate? How will you make your employer notice that you, the bearer of the solution to all his problems, are available and ready to be hired?

The Résumé

Traditionally, when seeking an interview, a résumé is expected of you. This is, after all, how you will provide your future employer with a summary of your job experiences. That said, only one out of a thousand résumés *do not* end up in the trash bin. Why? The résumé provides the employer with information as to where you've been and what you've done in the past. However, smart employers are more interested in the *now* and in the *future*. More than learning about what you've done before, they want to know what you are capable of doing for them now. They want to know what other things you may be capable of doing for them in the future. In other words, they are keener on learning about skills, abilities, and personal qualities that make you suitable for the task at hand. In interview lingo, this is what the term *qualifications* means.

As mentioned, successful interviews shed the spotlight on the needs of one's future employer rather than on one's own needs. The same applies to résumés. Therefore, to secure an interview, you must prepare a résumé that:

- describes your abilities instead of listing your job responsibilities;

- contains performance indicators, which demonstrate your competence;

- enumerates your accomplishments instead of tasks;

- starts off with an objective statement.

The latter must show how you plan to cater to the needs of the employer.

To understand more clearly, look at the example below:

Objective: To gain a position as an Obstetric Nurse

Does this objective say anything about you?

More importantly, does this objective say anything about how you will be of use to the employer?

The answer to both questions is a resounding NO. With such an objective, you are simply stating the obvious: That you want a job. But as mentioned in the previous chapter, that's not what employers want to hear. Now, take a look at this more elaborately-written objective:

Objective: Seeking an opportunity to utilize my skills and education in Obstetric Nursing in a career environment that provides a consistent and solid career path.

Does this objective say anything about you? Yes, it does. It communicates that you are a *qualified* professional who is looking for a suitable job that will provide you with a steady income and security in the future.

However, does this objective say anything about *how you will benefit the employer*?

Remember that you are not the one who sets the definition of the word "qualified." It is the employer who decides this in his own terms.

Now, consider this more effectively-written example:

Objective: To gain a position where my 10 years' worth of experience in Obstetric Nursing and 5 years as a CNM, can become an asset for the institution.

This is a lot better since it shows what the applicant can offer the employer. However, what would be even better is if you can translate all this *experience* into *qualifications*:

Objective: To become an *active member of* a healthcare institution that *needs* my 15 years of *managing* cases of high-risk pregnancies as well as my specialized skills as a CNM, including *delivering* neonatal resuscitation.

Of all the objectives, the last one sells the applicant best. For one thing, it features skills that not all nurses have.

Notice the use of these powerful verbs: "managing" and "delivering", and see how they speak volumes about the applicant's capabilities. It shows an applicant who can *manage*. It shows an applicant who can *deliver*. That's more appealing than an applicant who merely "carries out" tasks. Also, take note of the term "needs." The moment the employer views this résumé, he will start seeing the applicant less as someone begging for a job and more as someone who is offering a potential solution to the hospital's problems/needs. Moreover, the phrase: "to become an active member of" communicates that the applicant has the makings of a team player.

Another main difference between the first objective example and the last one is that the former specified a target job position (OB Nurse). The applicant does this without taking into consideration the possibility that the healthcare institution may not have an available slot for such a position. On the other hand, when you write a résumé that emphasizes your skills, the employer may consider offering you an alternative position that is also suitable for your qualifications.

Classified Ads

A classified ad is like a fishing net, which employers cast into the sea of potential workers so they can:

- catch possible candidates for an interview

- filter the entrants so they can get rid of 95% of them

Even so, your chances for landing an interview when writing in response to a job listing is greater compared to when you send out an unsolicited résumé. To maximize your chances of snagging an interview through a classified ad, do the following:

- Send in a response as quickly as possible, preferably within 24-48 hours after the release of the ad.

- Write a cover letter that is brief and goes directly to the point. In the initial sentence of your cover letter, include the source of the ad as well as the date. After that, express your interest in the position. State that you are interested because you believe that it matches your qualifications.

Example: Your advertisement for a computer engineer in the (state date) issue of (state source) interests me because my qualifications matches precisely with what you are looking for.

After that, proceed with your qualifications, which are of course, paraphrased versions of the qualifications stated in the ad.

Important: When responding to classified ads, make sure that you address only the qualifications mentioned in the ad. While you may be capable of offering so much more, just stick to what the employer is explicitly asking for. Otherwise, you might end up persuading the hiring manager that you're not a good fit for the job.

- Likewise, make sure that you address *every single criterion* stated by the employer even if it means tweaking some words a bit. If you're incapable of meeting all qualifications, your response will immediately end up in the garbage.

Example: If a listing asks for someone who is capable of installing, configuring, and customizing third-party scripts and you don't know how to do any of these things, don't ignore this criteria. Instead, write down: *Interested in* installing, configuring, and customizing third-party scripts.

You should be able to sell yourself to a prospective employer at a single glance. For this reason, you'll need to arrange your qualifications in bullet points. The harder the employer works to find out more about you, the better.

Some ads may ask you to include your salary requirements. The best move would be to not include it at all. If it can't be avoided, refrain from providing a specific figure. Simply refer to it instead.

Example: As I have continuously moved upward from one position to another, my rates have increased correspondingly.

You may also choose to provide a range.

Example: If you're hoping for $90,000 but would willingly to go for $85,000, then indicate your range as: $85,000 - $95,000, and then add the tasteful phrase: "depending on the extent of my duties."

In the succeeding chapters, more about how to handle the subject of compensation in job interviews will be discussed.

The Cold Call

When looking for a job, you don't have to wait around for the perfect ad to come your way. A cold call is when an applicant calls the company directly and conducts an employment query over the phone. The HR department serves as a filter that screens applicants and discards the "unwanted applicants" to make things easier for the hiring manager. When applying for larger companies, you usually make your cold call to the HR department. That said, one advantage of the cold call is that it's possible for you to skip the filter and go straight to the one person who has the power to hire you.

Naturally, this technique will work only if you've performed thorough research about the company that you're applying for. If you can't find the name of that person online, then one trick you can do is to call the HR department in the guise of someone conducting career research. Tell the HR department that you need to speak with the manager of the company and ask how you can get in touch with him/her. Make sure that you emphasize that you're not someone applying for a job, but rather you're someone who is simply looking for information.

Upon contacting the hiring manager, greet him/her. State your name. Follow up with: "____ suggested that I give you a call." What if no one recommended you per se? What if you got the hiring manager's number from HR? Then use these not-so-untruthful words: *"Your HR people suggested that I contact you."*

Now that you've cast the fishing line, it's time to hook the employer. Proceed with a statement that would interest him/her.

Example: "As you are well aware, Mr./Ms./Mrs. _____, a large majority of readers these days prefer electronic versions of reading materials. However, I see this as an opportunity rather than a problem..."

Next, tell your employer what you can do for him/her. Tell the hiring manager about your qualifications. As stated, this doesn't mean that you have to just talk about your past experience. Instead, emphasize your skills and your achievements.

Now to make that interview happen: *"I would very much welcome an opportunity to chat with you face-to-face so that I can share my strategies for increasing your company's sales. I believe it will benefit your business as it had benefited the previous company that I had worked with."*

At this point, your main goal is to arrange a meeting with the hiring manager. If you fail in this objective, the next best thing you can do is to persuade the manager to read your résumé. If this too fails, then at least ask the manager about similar job positions in other places. Alternatively, you may ask about other employment options in the same company.

End the call by prompting the hiring manager to take action.

Example:

"I will drop by your office at any time that is most convenient for you."

"I'll call you later this week so we can decide on a good time for us to get together."

Practice your confident, persuasive voice. Make your voice sound deeper since it commands more respect.

Speak slowly so that each word has value. According to a 2015 article in *The Journal of Psychological Science* (reprinted later in Business Insider Australia), employers are able to perceive your intelligence just by listening to the sound of your voice. In a research study conducted by Schroeder and Epley (Booth School of Business, University of Chicago), a group of student job applicants were asked to deliver a brief pitch to their target companies. The same pitch was to be delivered both verbally and in writing. Judges who were able to listen to the applicants' pitches rated them higher than the judges who only read written versions of the pitch. The point: You get a better chance of being hired if the hiring manager can actually listen to your pitch as opposed to just reading it.

Agencies

Do you want to know the reason why so many people fail to get jobs despite the aid of employment agencies? That's because the principal purpose of employment agencies is *not* to ensure that you land a job. Their primary purpose is to provide employers with the right employees for their companies. See the difference?

As mentioned earlier in this book, it's not about you. It's never about you. It's always about the company, the employer, or the job. For this reason, when you present yourself at an employment agency, do it as though you are presenting yourself in front of the employer himself. Be precise about the kind of job(s) that you're looking for and the kind of work that you think you are suited for. The agent is not your job counselor so don't treat him like one.

Don't slack off as though signing up with an agency means that it's only a matter of time before you get a job. Instead, sign up with other agencies too. Better yet, keep hunting for jobs on your own as well. Don't feel the least bit guilty about receiving multiple job offers. While you are advised to focus on the needs of the company during résumé writing and the interview, in the end, you mustn't forget to consider your own needs. After all, isn't this the reason why you're trying to get a job in the first place?

Lastly, if you believe that being with an agency is not doing you any good (ex. if you feel as though they're limiting your options), then understand that you have the freedom to walk away. When it comes to getting a job, the only person you can truly rely on to speak and act in your best interests is yourself.

Chapter 3: Receive an Interview Invitation like a True Professional

So you've received an invitation for a job interview. You must be ecstatic! Or possessed with sheer fear. This is the point where you start doubting yourself. This is where your excited optimism starts to blend with panic so that you wouldn't know where one begins and the other ends. Relax. At this phase, your *time* becomes your most precious asset so don't waste it by focusing on your emotions. Instead, concentrate on how you could increase your chances of acing the interview by receiving the invitation like a true professional.

The first step would be to issue a prompt response. Before that, however, make sure that you've checked or re-checked your schedule for that day. Unless absolutely necessary, re-scheduling is a no-no. Employers are looking for people who are organized and dependable. They are unlikely to warm up to candidates who show little regard for their time and efforts.

When you receive the invitation by phone, receive it calmly and in a business-like tone, even when inside, you feel like yelling and jumping up and down. Make sure that your voice is loud and clear enough to be heard on the line. Think before you speak so you that you ensure that you use proper grammar. If your resume was well-written (and for an employer to call, it must have been), then he/she is expecting you to be well-spoken as well. To prove otherwise would be disappointing. Make sure that you talk in complete sentences and strive to avoid lengthy pauses.

Smile and stand upright. The latter provides you with confidence and this will be evident in your voice. While the person at the end of the line may not be able to see you, smiling over the phone will aid in adding a hint of natural warmth in your tone.

Important: The phone call may, in itself, be a form of a preliminary screening interview prior to a face-to-face interview. So manage your emotions and pay close attention to the questions that the caller is asking. Even when it's not an initial interview, treat it like one. Write down all of the information that the caller is giving you. Don't put the phone down until you have gathered the following pertinent data:

- the name of the caller and his/her position/title in the company;

- the company's name;

- the date and time and the venue for the interview;

- the name(s) of the interviewer(s);

- the contact number(s) of the person(s) you will be meeting with on that day.

Don't hesitate to ask for directions. Here's a professional way of requesting them:

"I'm afraid I'm not very familiar with that area. Is it possible for you to tell me the best ways to get there from _____?"

One of the greatest mistakes that interviewees make is to show up late for interviews because they couldn't find the location. If possible, locate and visit the spot a day or days before the interview. This way, you can accurately calculate the amount of time needed to get there, get an idea of the traffic situation in the area, etc.

How should you end the conversation?

The smartest way would be to do it by repeating vital information to the caller. This way, he/she can correct any mistakes.

Example: *"I'll be at (address of the venue) on (date of the interview) at (time of the interview) and look for (contact person(s) or interviewer)."*

If you're already speaking with your future interviewer, then your closing statement should convey how you're looking forward to the meeting.

Example: *"Very well, Mr./Ms./Mrs. _____, I shall look forward to meeting you at (address of the venue) on (date of the interview) at (time of the interview). Thank you so much for calling."*

What if the interviewer/caller sets a schedule and you're not sure if you're available on that date/time?

If you're anticipating a call from a potential employer, you should always have a calendar, a pen, and a paper on hand. If, somehow, you're still caught unprepared, then inform the caller that you will call again to confirm your availability on that date/time.

You need to make the return call as soon as possible. Also, when doing this, make sure that you provide a specific time which you, of course, must follow.

Example: *"I need to consult my calendar. It's 9:30 a.m. now. Is it possible for me to call you back in half an hour, around 10 a.m. today?"*

What if you're *sure* that you can't make it at the appointed time?

Then say so. Your unavailability does not warrant an explanation.

Wrong: *"I'm sorry, but I can't have the interview on Wednesday because I have to..."*

Correct: *"I'm afraid I won't be able to have the interview on Wednesday. Any time before or after that is fine with me."*

Once you've both decided on a convenient date and time, try your best not to reschedule. That said, sometimes emergencies just come up. If you really, *really* need to reschedule an interview, then the best you can do is to minimize the damage by presenting your reason in the best possible light.

Example: In case of "professional emergencies," say something like:

"I sincerely apologize for any inconvenience this may cause you. However, I just cannot let the rest of my colleagues down."

You may have gained a negative point by getting the interviewer entangled in your scheduling conflict, but at least this statement gives evidence to your professional dedication and excellent moral character.

Receiving an Interview Invitation While At Work

What if you're looking for a new job without the knowledge of your current manager? What if the caller tries to contact you while you're at the workplace?

In such situations, any of the following responses may be appropriate:

"Can you give me a minute? I just need to close the door."

You don't have to explain why. You need only say that the conversation must be kept confidential. If the caller is just as professional as you are, then he won't pry. Don't mention that you're looking for job interviews behind your boss's back or that you're afraid your boss will fire you when he finds out you're looking for a new job. This communicates two things: disloyalty to your boss and fear of your current employer. Neither of these things will make you attractive to future employers.

What if you work in a cramped workspace where you can practically hear your colleague-from-the-next-compartment's breathing?

In such cases, it would be alright to say:

"Can you give me a minute? Let me move to someplace more private."

"I'm sorry, Mr./Ms./Mrs. _____. I'm afraid I'm not in a position to speak about the issue right now. Will it

be possible for me to call you back later at six o'clock this evening?"

Make it a point to call back within the day.

When expecting calls like these, you should already have a sound plan as to how and where you would receive the call (ex. in your parked car).

Important: If you're looking for job interviews while you're still employed, it would be best to practice discretion. Refrain from disclosing this sensitive information even to your closest colleagues. The knowledge that you're hunting for a new job may make you appear disloyal in the eyes of your current employer. If you end up not getting that target position after all, things could end up badly for you in your current workplace.

Scheduling the Interview

If the caller provides you with the freedom to schedule the interview, the best time would be before or around ten o'clock in the morning.

In a research study done by Frieder, Van Iddekinge, and Raymark (2015), it was established that the timing of an interview is a significant factor in how quickly the interviewer arrives at a decision about an interviewee. While dealing with the first few interviewees, the examiners have fewer information that they need to process.

This enables them to create a decision about the applicant's suitability more easily and more quickly. As they start interviewing more and more applicants, the amount of data that they need to recall and process and compare also increases, making decision-making more challenging. Thus, they are compelled to follow the heuristic method for judging the compatibility of the interviewees with the job position. This includes making use of educated guesses, stereotyping, and relying on one's intuition.

The 2015 study was carried out by analyzing data from hundreds of actual job interviews that took place at a university job fair. The bottom line: If you have your interview earlier in the morning, you'll be able to catch interviewers at a time when they are more alert and attentive.

As lunchtime approaches, examiners begin to feel distracted with other thoughts such as hunger, food cravings, errands to run at noon break, etc. Similarly, if you schedule your interview in the late afternoon, this is the time when the interviewer's energy level is at its lowest. For the same reasons, you also need to refrain from scheduling your interview during the seasons where the company is at its busiest. Again, this stresses the importance of conducting research about your target company, and that includes knowing its most eventful seasons.

Chapter 4: The Planning and Preparation Phase

Sufficient planning and preparation lends an interviewee the confidence that he/she needs to succeed in the interview.

Reflect on How You Perceive Yourself

What do you think you look like through the eyes of your future employer?

What are your key abilities? How do you display them? How did you make use of them at your previous job?

Do you possess any transferable skills? More importantly, will the employer be able to recognize these skills through the information that you've given him?

Transferrable skills refer to flexible skills that you can use in a variety of jobs as opposed to skills that are exclusive to a specific job position. Such skills are relevant to numerous areas of life and not just to one's professional life. Examples of transferrable skills include leadership skills, communication skills, numeracy skills, and problem-solving skills. Now, just about everyone you know may claim to possess such skills. That said, the trick lies in showing your future employer how your transferrable skill set can be useful for his business.

Consider this statement:

"I have good managerial skills."

It may sound alright, but claiming to have "good managerial skills" does not allow you to do a great job of selling yourself.

Consider this other statement:

"I am a manager."

A manager, unfortunately, is a job position and not a transferrable skill.

The thing is, you have the idea, but you don't know the best way to present it to your would-be employer. So how do you do it then? How do you transform your message from "I need a job." to "Your company needs me."?

Answer: Instead of using nouns and adjectives to describe your skills, use verbs. Use action words. Hence: "I *manage.*"

But what exactly do/did you manage?

The important thing you need to know about transferrable skills is that they can be categorized into three groups:

- skills concerning people

- skills concerning information

- skills concerning things

Now answer this: To which do you apply your transferrable skills to?

If the answer is people, then your transferrable skill is this:

"I manage people."

Another thing you need to reflect on is the gaps in your CV. What did you do during that time? More importantly, how would you explain it to your prospective employer in such a way that would benefit him (and in turn, benefit you)?

Firstly, when writing your CV, it's perfectly fine to just write down the year instead of the specific months. This way, your employer won't be too distracted by the gaps. This will enable him to concentrate on the rest of your CV.

When it comes to explaining gaps, honesty is almost always the best policy. That is, assuming that you've spent your time on worthy pursuits (ex. travelling, tending to your loved ones, etc.). That said, no matter how well your objectives were, you still need to present them in such a way that they would seem advantageous to your employer. In other words, everything that you write down in your CV must, in one way or another, serve to further your career or at least demonstrate your willingness to further your career (ex. while taking the time off to tend to your kids, mention that you ran a successful blog related to your trade, or that you worked freelance, or that you attended a handful of seminars or trainings pertaining to your field.)

The key is to be proactive.

Wrong: *"I've spent the past few months travelling."*

Correct: *"I took eight months off to immerse myself in various cultures. I believe this has allowed me to develop fresh perspectives and gain valuable life lessons. And now, I am more prepared than ever to re-focus on my career."*

Refrain from lying outright about a gap (ex. extending your time spent in a job position.) Hiring managers are hiring managers for a reason. They just might call up your references to check up on you.

Reflect on How You Perceive Your Employer

As mentioned previously, part of preparing for an interview is digging up some information about your target employer/company. You live in the age of easily-accessible information, so there's no reason why you won't be able to perform research.

More than researching about basic information (ex. the goods and services that the company offers), dig in a little deeper and find out how the company is doing financially. Who are its major competitors? What are the major problems that the industry is facing? Is it a hierarchical organization or a dynamic enterprise?

If it's a public company, peruse the company's annual reports. Follow the company's website or the business's social media pages. Just by looking at the ads that the company releases in magazines, newspapers, or on the Internet, you'll have an idea about how the company wants to project itself to the public.

Again, ask yourself: *Which of my talents and skills would this company need?* In other words: *Which of my skills should I put emphasis on to better sell myself to this company?*

Now, to show your interviewer that you have indeed done your research on the company, include phrases like these as you answer questions in your interview:

"I've always dreamt of being a part of an institution that has (insert important bit of company's history here.)"

"I believe that my broad experience in (insert company's goods/services here) makes me a suitable fit for your company."

"I believe these skills that I've mentioned would be beneficial to your company's current goal, which is to _____."

"I understand that one of the major challenges in the industry today is _____. I believe I may have a solution to this problem."

"My personal philosophy is in line with the company's philosophy, which is _____."

"As we're both aware, the company is in need of _____. I am prepared to offer my services as part of the solution."

"I believe my knowledge in _____ and _____ can assist in realizing the company's vision, which is _____."

For better impact, you may use these in the introduction or in the concluding statement of your answers.

Determine the Possible Areas of Questioning

Use your prediction skills to anticipate the questions that the interviewer(s) are most likely to ask you. You can get some clues just by looking at the job descriptions or requirements

Example: If the job ad calls for stock handlers to work in a warehouse and to check stocks, then you'll know that the employers want individuals who are physically fit and have good numeracy skills. Thus, you must prepare to be asked questions about your health. You also know that numerical competence and knowing how to drive and lift equipment can give you extra points. You know you'll have to sell these skills to your interviewer. You also know that since a stock handler will be handling valuable goods, then trustworthiness and honesty are among the top personality traits that the employer will be looking for. Hence, you know that you need to project these qualities to the interviewer during the meeting.

The three major areas of questioning are the following. Expect to be asked questions about these things:

Qualifications

The interviewer does not want you to give him a list of all the training courses you've attended in the past. He wants to know what you've learned from them, and more importantly, how the things you learned can be of measureable benefit to the company. Before the interview, think about the most valuable lessons you've learned from these courses and summarize them in a couple of sentences. Again, use action words that will appeal the most to the employer's business/organization.

Example: Don't say you've attended a seminar about good salesmanship. Instead, say you've attended courses that enabled you to *persuade* customers to *purchase* the company's products and therefore *increase* the company's sales.

Persuade. Purchase. Increase. These are exactly the things the interviewer wants to hear from you.

Do mention measurable achievements such as examinations that you've passed and awards that you've received.

Past Work Experience

Don't assume that the interviewer is already familiar with the duties and responsibilities of a person in your previous position. For instance, don't just say "I worked as a filing clerk" and expect the interviewer to understand that you've had experience in handling legal documents.

That said, refrain from enumerating all of your tasks in your previous position. Instead, ask yourself: *Which of these tasks make me marketable to the employer? Which of these tasks are relevant to his business/company?*

Example: "In my five years as a filing clerk, I've become skilled at filing documents *according to number*."

This will emphasize that you have great numeracy skills. This is great if you're applying for a position that deals with numbers on a daily basis.

Don't just concentrate on specific tasks. Reflect on your actual job experiences and recall the moments of glory where you have proved to yourself and to your past employer how capable you are. See how you can present this to your future employer in a way that would make you seem valuable to his company/business. For instance, talk about the time when you had to trace missing documents or retrieve records under time pressure.

These are your so-called "war stories" which you will have to share with the interviewer when he asks you questions in the line of: *"What's the most challenging situation you've encountered at work?"* Write these stories down. Then, rehearse and memorize how you would tell each story to the interviewer.

Remember: The main reason why your interviewer will be asking you about your past work experience is not because he wants to know where you've been. Rather, he wants to know what great things you have done for your previous company and whether you'll be able to do these things for him too. In other words, he wants to have a clear idea as to what kind of employee you would be. He wants to know whether or not he'll regret investing in you.

Personality/Character

As mentioned, most employers value personality more than skills and work experience. This is why, when asked about your "best qualities" or your "most outstanding traits", you must not focus on specific technical skills but rather on your personality. After all, any technical skills that you possess have already been written down on your CV and there is no need for redundancy during the interview. According to a study conducted by Dodaj (Department of Psychology,

56

University of Mostar) in 2012, personality traits are linked to certain working traits as well as organizational consequences, such as motivation, leadership, and productivity. The research suggests that even a potential employee's ability to fake positive personality traits reflects his ability to fine-tune his personality as needed to thrive in the work environment.

What should you bring with you to the interview?

When it comes to interviews, here is another common myth that needs to be debunked:

Interviewers come fully prepared for the task at hand.

On the contrary, most interviewers don't have a clue as to what they're doing at all. Some dread the prospect of having to sit for hours in the interview room just as you do. When an interviewer comes unprepared, this places you at a disadvantage. An interviewer who's just winging it will end up asking standard, uninteresting questions, which will minimize your opportunity to showcase your skills. In other words, the interviewer's boring and incompetent questions will make *you* look boring and incompetent.

An inadequately-prepared interviewer can undermine all your efforts in preparing for the interview. Therefore, ensuring that the interview flows smoothly is not just the job of the interviewer. It is also *your* job to make sure that the conversation keeps going at a lively pace. The good news is that you can have the power to steer the course of the dialogue in a way that would be most beneficial for you.

As previously mentioned, employers want potential employees to be bearers of solutions, not problems. Right now, *you're his problem*. The interview is his problem. Be a bringer of a solution by making the interview easy for him.

Don't just tell them. Show them.

An *interview kit* comprises of extra copies of your resume (in case your interviewer forgot to bring his copy of your resume), recommendation letters, and other visual tools to showcase your knowledge and skills, such as pictures of equipment you've handled, business presentation copies, your art portfolio featuring your best work, etc. The interview kit not only provide you with an interesting and effective way to sell your skills, but it also provides both you and the interviewer with a conversational piece, which will inspire further discussion. This will prevent the dialogue from going stale.

As your interviewer looks through the interview kit, explain its contents in such a manner that would help you promote yourself.

Example: *"This is the thank-you note that I received when I helped a client save up to $500,000 with the system that I developed."*

This will catch the interviewer's interest and he'll ask you to tell him more about that. This is more productive and advantageous for the both of you rather than spending the rest of the interview talking about your hobbies or the gaps in your CV.

Important: The interview kit belongs to you. It must communicate the idea that your precious designs/ideas/concepts will be available to the employer *once he hires you*. Thus, refrain from leaving it at the hands of the interviewer for his perusal. Instead, allow him to just have a look at it and refrain from making the interview kit the center of the whole interview.

Ask

Another thing you have to bring with you to the interview room is this: *Questions.*

During an interview, the job interviewer may prompt *you* to ask questions (ex: *Do you have anything you'd like to ask me?)* When the tables are turned, how should you respond then?

Asking questions during an interview provides you with an opportunity to discover important details about the job or the company that you're trying to be a part of. Applicants who do not ask questions provide the interviewer with the impression that they're not that interested in the job or in the organization. Moreover, interviewees who ask questions are perceived by employers as more intelligent compared to those who choose to remain silent. Thus, it is essential that you prepare at least two questions prior to the interview. More than that, you must make a mental list of more potential questions to ask in case both of your questions have already been answered during the course of the conversation.

Important: Your questions at the end of the interview can make or break your acceptance into your dream job. If you end up asking a question with an answer that you are already expected to know or has already been covered in the interview, the interviewer will see you as someone who is inattentive or slow to catch on. Simply put, refrain from asking questions just for the sake of asking them. Each question you ask must be of value to you, and if possible, to your interviewer too.

Examples:

How has this position evolved?

This will give you an idea as to whether you're applying for a job with a future or one that is practically a dead-end.

How would you describe the culture of this company?

This will show that you're interested in the company. At the same time, you'll get an idea as to whether that company is a good fit for you.

Who do you think are your major competitors? What advantages do you have over them?

Asking this gutsy question shows that you're already thinking up ways on how to help the company obtain its goals and beat the competition.

What skills or experiences should an ideal aspirant have for this job?

In case the interview mentioned a skill that you haven't been able to include in your list, you'll still have a chance to cover it.

Do you have any reservations regarding my qualifications?

While this questions places you at a vulnerable position, this also shows that you are extremely confident about your own skills. Furthermore, if the interviewer *does* have hesitations about your qualifications, you'll be provided with an opportunity to redeem yourself.

Remember: Whatever questions you ask the interviewer, it should have the following goals:

- ensure that the interviewer has no hesitations about you or your qualifications;

- show your interest in the job and in the company;

- determine whether the job or the company is a good fit for you.

If you want the part, dress for it

Dressing up for an interview is not just about looking organized and smart. Sure, it's that too. But more importantly, it is about looking like you're someone who actually *belongs* in the target company. Dressing the part will aid the interviewer in visualizing you working for the company alongside existing employees. This will help lift any doubts as to whether or not you're suited for the position.

This means that before the interview, it is essential that you do your research on the company's culture. You can easily find out about the office's dress code by observing the organization's current employees. If you're moving up, make sure you dress for the position that you're seeking and not for the one you're in now. This also means that business outfits aren't always perfect for all types of job interviews. Rather than wearing an outfit that is "fashionable" or "formal", focus on looking for something that is *appropriate,* something that says: "I fit in."

Tip: As a professional, you hardly need to be lectured about the more obvious aspects of grooming. That said, apart from ensuring that your clothes are clean, neatly-pressed, and well-fitted to your body type, you must refrain from using too much perfume or aftershave. The sense of smell is strongly linked with emotions. A scent that is too strong will make you appear inconsiderate and intrusive, not to mention unlikable, if the interviewer happens to hate the scent. As mentioned, face-to-face interviews are inevitably subjective. Use your favorite scent cautiously and sparingly.

Chapter 5: What To Do While Waiting

Arrive early

Almost every interview-related book and article will tell you how important punctuality is. You are certainly expected to be on time on the day of the interview. The surest way to avoid tardiness is to arrive at the venue at least 30 minutes ahead of your scheduled interview time. But what will you do with all this time in your hands? Do you spend it nursing the little butterflies fluttering in your stomach?

Use the time productively by observing the reception area

Look for company-related literature, which are likely to contain their annual reports, brochures of their products and services, and their newsletters. Determine the business's flagship product and the recent events that the company took part in. This way, you'll get to stock up on your knowledge of the company or the trade.

Converse with the receptionist

If no such literature is available, and if the receptionist isn't too busy, you can *casually* squeeze some useful information out of him/her. Greet the receptionist. Introduce yourself and ask for his/her name. Ask him/her how he/she is doing. Too often, applicants regard receptionists as room fixtures, which is a huge mistake because as an inside person, a receptionist can be a valuable ally.

Example:

Applicant: *"Hello. I'm _____. I'm scheduled to see Mr./Mrs./Ms. _____ at _____ ."*

Receptionist: *"Please have a seat..."*

Applicant: *"Thank you. And your name is..?"*

Receptionist: (name)

Applicant: *"Hello, (call receptionist by name). How are you doing?"*

Receptionist: *"I'm fine, thanks."*

Applicant: *"I have an interview with _____. So, how is he/she today?"*

Receptionist: *"Oh, well, a bit stressed. You know how it is..."*

Applicant: *"I see. Anything out of the ordinary?"*

Receptionist: *"Well, it's just that the annual sales meeting is almost upon us again. Things always get pretty tense during this time of the year."*

See how being friendly could make all the difference?

Now you know what your interviewer's current mood is. Now you know what your potential employer's present problem is. This means you can now think of how you'll be able to make him see that you are capable of easing his load.

Example:

"Mr./Mrs./Ms. _____, thank you so much for seeing me. I appreciate your time, especially since I know how busy you are with your sales meetings. I understand completely what that's like."

Now, *this* is a way to make a grand entrance.

Another advantage of being friendly with the receptionist is that knowing you by name makes it more likely for him/her to prioritize your follow-up call after the interview.

Calm the Butterflies

Even before you enter the interview room, be aware of your body and control all voluntary and involuntary gestures, which may subconsciously communicate fear and nervousness. Nervous body language reveals your lack of confidence. Moreover, the interviewers won't appreciate you making them feel terrible about themselves. After all, you're going to an interview, not into a monster's lair. Stop doing the following:

- twirling your hair

- licking your lips

- biting your nails

- swinging your legs

- tapping your foot

- touching your nose

- touching your mouth

- wringing your hands

When you allow your body to exhibit any of these outward signs of anxiety, it further convinces your subconscious that you are indeed anxious.

What if your interviewer is late?

The worst thing you can do is to just sit there and well... wait. When you arrive at the venue, make sure that you check in with the receptionist so your interviewer knows that you have arrived.

If there is no receptionist present, then wait until one minute after the exact time. For this reason, you have to make sure that your clock is in sync with the office's clock. Next, walk towards the interviewer's door and knock.

Five minutes after the scheduled time, approach the receptionist and ask if he/she has had any word from the interviewer.

Example: *"I'm scheduled for an interview at (exact time). Have you heard from Mr./Ms./Mrs. _____?"*

At twenty minutes past the scheduled time, approach the receptionist again and request that he/she check in with your interviewer.

Example: *"I wonder if it might be possible for you to check in with Mr./Mrs./Ms. _____ . He/she is quite late."*

One hour after the scheduled time, get a piece of paper and a pen (you should be carrying these) from your folder/attaché and then write a note for the interviewer.

Example:

Dear Mr./Mrs./Ms. _____,

It is (state exact time), an hour past the scheduled interview time. This has left me to assume that you have been detained by some unavoidable and unexpected circumstance. Perhaps it would be best if we re-schedule the interview. You may reach me at (your number). I shall check in with you later this afternoon.

Sincerely,

(your name)

Fold the note and then hand it over to the receptionist. Politely ask the receptionist to make certain that the interviewer receives the letter. No matter how you choose to write your letter, make sure that you keep it polite and professional. There must be no hint of anger, disappointment, or annoyance.

What if the interviewer finally does show up?

If this happens, then proceed with the interview and forget everything. It will do you absolutely no good to go into an interview with a chip on your shoulder. Chances are, your interviewer has a perfectly good reason for being late. That said, he is under no obligation to explain the details to you. Moreover, depending on the circumstance, you should reflect too on whether or not it would be fine for you to work for an employer who thinks nothing of keeping his subordinates waiting for him.

Chapter 6: Making a Brilliant First Impression

In interviews, communication begins way before the first word passes from your/the employer's lips. About 75% of the communication during the interview is done through an exchange of non-verbal cues. A quick visual once-over from your interviewer is enough to tell him/her a lot about you and the kind of employee you would be.

- As far as first impressions are concerned, height *does* make a huge impact. Height suggests authority and commands respect. So stand up straight and walk tall the moment you enter the interview room.

- Don't forget to smile. Moderately. To avoid the negative impression caused by an obviously fake smile, visualize a pleasant scene in your mind like walking through a garden.

- Establish eye contact with the employer the moment you enter the room. This is the quickest way to connect with him/her. It conveys honesty, confidence, and respect.

- If the interviewer shakes your hand, make sure that your palms aren't sweaty. Mirror your interviewer's grasp. Hold his hand a fraction of a second longer than you mean to. Make sure that you maintain eye contact during the handshake. Finally, before you let go of the interviewer's hand, begin talking (example: "It's great to finally meet you." or "I'm happy to be here.")

- Allow your interviewer to be the first one to be seated. Not only is this the polite thing to do, this will also provide the interviewer with a change to quite literally look up to you. In this brief moment, the interviewer will feel a sense of your authority.

- Sit across the interviewer. If you have a choice, select a seat with a straight back over seats with soft cushions. The latter will only tempt you to slouch while the former will enable you to sit up straight. What's more, sitting in over-sized chairs have a tendency you make you appear small and vulnerable.

- Once you're both seated, allow the interviewer to speak first and listen attentively as he does.

Important: There are times when you might come across an interviewer who would remain silent just so he could see how you would handle the situation. If the interviewer is just sitting there, looking at you, resist the urge to fidget, to touch your hair, or adjust your tie, etc. Don't look away out of self-consciousness. Instead, just look at him in the eye with an eager, anticipatory expression and a smile. Avoid prolonging the silence by taking the lead.

When the interviewer is silent because he is looking at your resume, tolerate the silence. However, when he is looking straight at you with the same eager, anticipatory expression through wide eyes and arched eyebrows and slightly open lips, this is your cue to help him out and lead the conversation. So how do you start? A simple question might work.

Example:

*"Have you **had the chance** to **examine** my résumé?"*

You'll be surprised to know that most interviewers neglect to read the applicants' résumés until during the actual interview.

Note: *"had the chance"* suggests that you understand how busy the interviewer is and that you're completely open to the idea that he/she has not read your CV at all. Meanwhile, using "examine" or "review" or "assess" shows that you assume that the reader has already read your resume and that you're in no way accusing him of being negligent.

If your interviewer responds with something like: *"I haven't had the chance to assess it as fully as I'd like to."* Then it's as good as getting a: *"Sorry, but no."* If such is the case, don't despair. Grab this as an opportunity to sell yourself.

Your best response would be something like this: *"Perhaps it would be more convenient if I state the highpoints of my qualifications."*

Then, use a relaxed and conversational tone to talk about your qualifications instead of merely enumerating your skills and experiences.

Another more gutsy way to get the conversation going is to focus on the employer's needs.

Example:

"How would you like me to work to increase the company's sales?"

Remember: In the interview room, brief moments of silence may seem to stretch out to eternity. That said, resist the urge to fill the silence with just about anything. Silence is more preferable than you blurting out nonsense or the conversation being redundant. In other words, think before you open your mouth.

Establish rapport within the limited amount of time you're given

Creating a social bond takes time but with the amount of time you're given for an interview, you need to work fast. One way you can create instant rapport is by using the pronouns "us", "we", and "our" in your statements. "I", "my", "you", and "yours" create an invisible, but palpable, barrier between the candidate and the interviewer.

Example: "I increased the sales at _____. I believe that it's possible for *us* to achieve the same result here."

All of a sudden, your interviewer gets a clear vision of the two of you working side by side.

Magic Phrases

The key phrases that you use during the interview can have a powerful impact on the interviewer.

To suggest that you're a great team player, use the words *collaborate, cooperate, team up, work together, interact, and brainstorm.*

To communicate understanding, use the following phrases: *"I appreciate...", "I understand...", and "exactly what I'm thinking..."*

To inspire a more relaxed atmosphere, use phrases like these: *"I was under the impression that...", "Perhaps we should talk this over so that...", "We might be able to agree that..."*

To prevent a foreseeable confrontation, use these phrases: *"Allow me to explain my thinking...", "I believe it's possible for us to seek alternatives..."*

Negative Phrases

Just as there are magic phrases, there are also phrases that you should *avoid* using throughout the interview. Here are a few examples:

"You're mistaken..."

"You don't get it..."

"What, exactly, are you trying to say?"

"I dislike..."

"I was right..."

Anything that would make the interviewer feel stupid, inferior, rude, or bad at his job must be avoided.

You must also avoid phrases that make it seem as though you're passing the blame to someone else (or to the interviewer):

"not my fault..."

"not my job..."

"none of my business..."

"He/she should have..."

"I had nothing to do with..."

Every word counts, so eliminate pointless and unnecessary words from your speech:

"sort of..."

"kind of..."

"you know?"

"right?"

"I guess..."

"What I'm actually trying to say is..."

Pay attention to what your body is saying

As the interview progresses, be conscious of what your body is doing. Use body language to maintain the rapport that you've built with the interviewer.

- To show him/her that you're listening very closely to what he or she is saying, tilt your head to one side.

- Refrain from raising your eyebrows as this communicates disbelief.

- Avoid narrowing your eyes because this hints at suspicion, anger, puzzlement, disagreement, or disapproval.

- A steady stare will make you appear arrogant and manipulative.

- Thrusting your chin out boldly may cause you to look arrogant. Meanwhile, a slight outward thrust of the chin may suggest confidence.

- When you unconsciously rub the back of your neck during an interview, this translates to impatience.

- Keep your palms open from the beginning of the interview to instantly convey trust and honesty.

- Avoid crossing your arms or your legs as this will make you seem defensive, uninterested, aggressive, or defiant.

Chapter 7: Be a Dynamic Listener and a Smart Speaker

Sell yourself like a pro

The job market today is more competitive than ever. Think of it this way:

It's easy to advertise a product when there are fewer competitors. All you need to do is to show the product to the consumer (example: show potential consumers an image of a bath soap and they'll buy it because they know what it's for.) However, if there are several similar products on the market, showing the consumers an image of the product is not enough to convince consumers to buy it. You have to remind them what it's for, how it will make their lives easier/better, and all the other reasons why they should buy it (this is when you start using commercial models, the perfect script, perfect background music, perfect packaging, etc.) More importantly, you have to show potential consumers why your product is better than all the others. It's for this reason why TV and printed ads strive to be more colorful, more interesting, and more unique.

And with the number of job-seekers out there, this is exactly how you should sell yourself as well.

What makes a great salesman great? It's when he's able to take control of the situation while making the clients believe that they're the ones in control. An experienced salesman will discuss the needs and concerns of the clients while persuading the customers that what he's selling is the answer to their problems.

A job interview is no different. View the interview as an opportunity to make a sale. You take control and then subtly guide the interviewer into making you a job offer. Your main goal during the interview is to transform yourself in the eyes of the interviewer from a total stranger to someone that his company must buy.

Listen actively

One of the greatest misconceptions about interviews is that it is the interviewee's moment in the spotlight where he can speak as much as he wants to about himself. On the contrary, active listening is twice as important as speaking in interviews. While a chatty candidate's enthusiasm to please the employer may seem amusing, it doesn't always result to a productive interview. Simply put, it's not about how much you say but how much value your words contain.

Listen closely to what the interviewer says about his business/organization. Your responses must be based according to his company's needs. This way, you turn from being a job applicant to a partner who's eager to share ideas and solutions.

Be on the lookout for conversation builders

From time to time, the interviewer will say some things that you can use to build an interesting conversation.

Example:

Interviewer: "The low inventory turnover is one of our biggest problems."

Applicant: "I understand completely. I've had experience in finding solutions for low inventory turnover in my previous position. Exactly what type of problems are you facing at the moment?"

Mirror

When you listen, don't just sit there like a cold marble statue. This would embarrass or offend your interviewer. Worse, it might send the message that you're not that interested in the job after all. Respond through your body language. Nod in agreement from time to time. That said, don't exaggerate your responses by agreeing to every single thing that the interviewer says. You must have your own opinions. Even so, restrain yourself and put your opinions on hold long enough to hear the interviewer out. You may not 100% agree with what the interviewer is saying, but play your cards right by finding a common ground and taking it from there.

Example:

Interviewer: "I think _____ is highly important. To accomplish this, we must use Approach A or Approach C."

Applicant: "I certainly agree that _____ is of primary importance. And I also favor approach C. While I can see the advantages of using Approach A, have you considered trying Approach B?"

Interviewer: "Why?"

Applicant: "Well, based from my experience, one of the greatest advantages of Approach B is…"

Lean forward slightly or sit at the edge of your seat to communicate to the interviewer that you find the exchange stimulating. Practice the art of mirroring the interviewer's message. This means that you match his/her tone. When he's excited about something, reflect his enthusiasm. When he adopts a serious tone while discussing a certain topic, reflect his seriousness.

Important: Limit your use of mirroring techniques, especially when it comes to mimicking your interviewer's body language.

It's true that mimicry may serve as a social glue that can assist in the promotion of rapport between human beings. In fact, years of research has proved that generally, subtly mirroring another person's tone, vocabulary, words, posture, and gestures can make you seem more likable to that individual. However, more than one recent study by psychological researchers reveal that when it comes to job interviews, mimicry must be kept to a minimum, especially when there is more than one interviewer.

In an experiment done by scientists from University of California, San Diego, several mock interviews were recorded. In the interviews, some of the participants mimicked the interviewers' gestures while others did not. After this, the scientists asked judges to watch the videos and measure the interviewees' level of competence, likeability, and credibility. The result? The judges found the candidates who kept mirroring to a minimum to be more competent, credible, and likeable.

A similar study was conducted by a team of experts at Texas Tech and Drew Universities. According to the study, mirroring can have negative effects on an applicant's success. This is because humans mimic not only positive gestures but also negative gestures as well. In other words, if your interviewer happens to find you less likeable or if he's just having a bad day, mirroring his gestures, his facial expression, or his tone of voice will only cause you to send a negative message to his subconscious. You become a living mirror of his negative emotions. Seeing you reflect how he's feeling inside will only serve to reinforce his negative perception of you.

Therefore, use mirroring strategies sparingly. Instead, concentrate on using body language to convey confidence and enthusiasm. You already have a lot on your mind during an interview and this is one less thing that you should worry about.

Repeat and rephrase

Rephrasing is one way to prove to the interviewer that you've been listening to him attentively. Like mirroring, rephrasing must be kept to a minimum. Make sure you restate only the most important points to the interviewer.

Example:

"If I understand you correctly…"

"From what I understand, you're saying that…"

Remind the interviewer why you're there in the first place

This may seem a bit frustrating, but in case the interviewer comes unprepared, his rambling thoughts may lead the conversation into an unpredictable path that will hinder you from selling yourself most effectively. At this point, your job is to give him a little nudge back to the right direction.

Example: *"I just can't tell you how excited I am to be here. I believe that what I have to offer could be of use to this company."*

With a statement like this, you're placing the focus back on the reasons why you're the right person for the job.

You might come across an interviewer who likes to monopolize the conversation. Should you butt in? Definitely. How else would you be able to have the opportunity to sell yourself?

But how do you interrupt a talkative interviewer's monologue without seeming rude?

First, absorb what you can from the interviewer's words. What you're actually listening in for are conversation builders and opportunities to highlight your selling points. Once it comes out of your interviewer's non-stop mouth, pounce on it.

Example:

Interviewer: *"As I was saying, one of the biggest challenges in this business is to guarantee sufficient cash flow--"*

Applicant: *"Allow me to interrupt you for a second. What you're saying is just too interesting. Management of cash flow is actually one of my main areas of interest. I have a couple of fresh ideas which you might be interested in hearing and I can't wait to hear your thoughts on them..."*

Another type of interviewer you might come across is the stressed out, overworked type. He/she may be distracted during the whole interview. He/she may even cut you short to answer phone calls. Instead of feeling indignant, express your sympathy. Then, use it as a way to bring up the value that you can add to the company.

Example:

"Wow, you really are very busy during this time of the year. I know what it's like and I can totally see why the company could use someone with my skills and experience."

This will direct the interviewer's attention back to you.

Remember: There are times when the job interviewing task falls on a chiefly technical person. When this happens, you get an interviewer who will lead the conversation into a discussion of technical matters. While it's important to demonstrate your technical know-how, it is also necessary to remember that this isn't all that your interviewer wants to know about you. Naturally, he'll also want to know what you would be like as an employee. Chances are, he may be having a hard time communicating what he really wants to ask you. The solution? Look for a way to connect your technical skills with your transferrable skills. Provide examples of situations where you used *both*.

Keep in mind the lessons that your high school teacher taught you

Whoever said that high school subjects have no practical application in real life wasn't familiar with the rules of successful interviews. Remember when your grammar school teacher kept hounding you about using a substantial topic sentence, an engaging introduction, and a powerful conclusion in your essays? Well, you have to follow the same rules when answering interview questions.

Open with your topic sentence. Then, proceed with statements that support the topic sentence. Finally, end with a conclusion that summarizes your point.

Example:

"I understand that it's my job to find out and cater to our potential clients' needs, which will, in turn, enable me to *increase* the company's sales. This is why I made it my business to help the company to *earn* _____ dollars in sales last quarter. I was able to *persuade* former clienteles such as _____ and _____ to *purchase* the company's most recent products. I also *secured* new clients such as _____ and _____. Moreover, I *collaborated* with

_____ and _____ departments to help draw more attention to the company's flagship product, which is _____, and thus, maximizing its visibility to potential consumers. **Within one year of being in the company, I increased the company's sales by _____ % through diligence, social skills, salesmanship abilities, and by being a team player."**

Phrases that Keep the Ball Rolling

Using the following magic phrases will aid in maintaining the momentum of the conversation:

"I agree..."

"I can certainly relate..."

"That's interesting..."

"We should talk about..."

"Tell me more..."

"We should pursue that further..."

"That's also one of my biggest concerns..."

There are also phrases that could stop a conversation dead in its tracks. Here are a few examples of what you must avoid:

"Definitely not..."

"I absolutely disagree..."

"There is no way..."

"It's impossible..."

"It's final..."

"That's not how it should be done..."

Be on the lookout for 'Buy Signals'

You'll know an interviewer is interested in you when he starts using phrases such as the following:

"Sounds great."

"Interesting."

"I like that!"

Buy signals like these are signs that you've successfully caught your employer with your hook. Now it's time for you to reel him in, proverbially speaking. You do this by expounding on the idea that captured his interest. That said, unless they're really, really impressed, interviewers are rarely expressive. Often, their buy signals come in the form of a request for you to elaborate further on the topic.

Example:

"Can you tell me more about…"

"I'd like to hear more about…"

"Let's go back to…"

"Would you care to be more specific about…"

Now, most interviewees would dread the idea of being asked to speak more about a certain topic. Since you're reading this book, you shouldn't be feeling this way any longer! This is an indicator that you've hit the right button. But what is the correct way of expounding on an idea?

As mentioned, in an interview, you have to think of yourself as a product. In marketing, a product's *features* refer to the characteristics of the product (ex: portable, compact, etc.) If you're a product, then your features are your skills (ex: great managerial skills, reliable, trustworthy, etc.) On the other hand, a product's *benefits* refer to the positive things that it can do for the user (ex: portable, compact materials can be used while on the go and are easy to store.)

It's your *features* that will catch the interviewer's attention. To draw him in, you now have to present your *benefits*. In other words: *How can your skills make the employer's business/life more profitable/better?*

Example:

"I believe that the most important part of my position as an assistant manager is to *provide you* with more *time* to pursue higher responsibilities. My goal is to support you in the management of the store so you can have more valuable time in your hands."

Make a closing statement that closes the sale

You're playing the part of a salesman. This means you're not leaving the interview room without urging the employer to seal the deal.

Wrong: *"So, did I get the job?"/"Did I do okay?"*

This comes across as overly presumptuous, pathetic, and perhaps worst of all, needy. You're likely to end up with the standard dismissive response: "Don't call us. We'll call you."

Correct:

"Based on all that I've told you, don't you think I would be a great fit for the company?"

This part can be quite tricky. You need to make use of a closing statement that will actually extract a positive answer from the employer. To use or not to use closing statements like this will depend on how well you've established rapport with your interviewer and how effectively you were able to answer the interview questions. If you have a good feeling about the interview, proceed to prompt the employer into action. If not, follow a different route:

"Thank you so much for your time, Mr./Mrs./Ms. _____. It has been a great pleasure and I do believe I have a great deal to offer to this institution. But please, if there's anything that I wasn't able to discuss to your satisfaction, do let me know. What could I tell you to encourage you to make a proposal?"

Keep in mind that it's not about pressuring the employer to make a decision on the spot. This is about increasing your chances of urging the employer to commit to you positively. Closing statements like these suggest a hint of urgency without the sense of impatience or desperation. It simply reminds the interviewer of your value.

Chapter 8: The Ten Most Important Interview Questions and How to Answer Them

There are literally hundreds of interview books out there that will offer you a list of interview questions and the "best" ways to answer them. You can memorize and rehearse the Q&A's, but what if you get asked that one crucial question that wasn't covered by the book? In truth, the "best" way to answer *any* kind of interview question is not to practice with an endless list of questions and answers but to *practice the way you think*. As mentioned at the beginning of this book, interview questions are one and the same. They come in various shapes and colors, but in the end, the interviewer is really asking you this one vital question: *"Why should we hire you?"*

1) Tell me something about yourself.

What the interviewer actually means is: *"What do you have to offer me?"*

Most interviewees believe that this is one of the most challenging questions an interviewer could ask. It is actually a great open-ended opportunity to share your best features. That said, resist the urge to praise yourself to the heavens. Keep it short and limit your answer to the features that you think will be most beneficial to the employer's business. For instance, you may have both technical computer skills and salesmanship skills. But if you're applying for a position which will require you to deal mostly with the technical aspect of computers, then stick to selling your computer skills.

Fight the inclination to present your whole autobiography. Instead, keep your answer short by providing a brief background and highlighting some of your most notable accomplishments. Connect your educational background with the current position that you're holding. Make sure you cover your educational and career background and your most recent job experience. It is important that you express how your career has taken a logical advancement.

"I grew up in Connecticut and moved to New York where I studied Fine Arts and Art History at NYU. Straight out of college, I got a job at as an art curator at ____. Working in this job allowed me to learn a great deal about my chosen field and to cultivate my skills and knowledge as well as my stamina, my social skills, and my salesmanship skills. From there, I was able to obtain a senior position at _____. That's where I was truly able to develop my managerial

skills as well as my ability to handle high-profile projects and manage budgets up to $1 million. Right now, I believe that all the skills and experiences that I've gathered throughout the years make me a suitable candidate for a position in your company. I intend to prove that today. Do tell me, what are the qualities you are seeking in an ideal applicant for this job position?"

With this answer, you were able to answer the interviewer's actual question: "What do you have to offer me?"

The things you are able to offer him are:

- your excellent stamina

- your social skills

- your salesmanship skills

- your managerial skills

- and your ability to manage million-dollar projects and budgets

2) Why do you want to work in this company?

Why indeed? While your true answer may be because you need something from the company (a salary, stability), make it seem as though it's the company that needs something from you.

For this question, mention the features of the company that appeal to you the most. Discuss how the company is the perfect place for you. In other words, show the interviewer why you will fit right in. Proceed to talk about the skills that you possess, which will enable you to benefit from the company while at the same time allowing the company to benefit from you. Demonstrate that you are eager for an opportunity to contribute.

"I'll go ahead and say right out that I'm thrilled with the idea of working in this company. I am seeking an opportunity where my skills will be put to good use and I think that this is the perfect place for me to apply and demonstrate my expertise. For instance, I am very interested in being a part of your company's current project: _____. I am positive that with my

experience in cutting costs and maximizing revenues,
I can contribute a great deal to this project's success."

3) What makes you certain that you're qualified for this position?

When answering questions like this, you need only to remember that your contribution to a company is often only measured through two things:

- Money

- Time

Therefore, show your interviewer how you can help your employer increase the value of either or both. Thinking of yourself as a product, this is the time where you answer the interviewer with your *benefits* as opposed to your *features.*

*"I believe that, considering my experience and skills in my previous job as a _____, I can aid you in saving time by ensuring that the workplace functions smoothly and productively. Coupled with my diligence and skills in negotiation, I also believe that I can lower **our** department's costs while increasing*

*the revenues. By implementing _____, I was able to increase the revenue of (name of previous company you've worked for) by up to 25% in just 4 months' time. I see no reason why I shouldn't be able to do a similar thing for this company, **should I be provided with the opportunity** to work here."*

4) Why did you leave your last job?

This can be translated to: If you were doing so well there, why did your employers allow you to leave? Is there anything about you that we should be wary of?

When answering questions similar to this, make it a point to present the facts as briefly as possible and to concentrate on the future. Don't dwell too long on the subject as this may cause your interviewer to grow suspicious. Emphasize that your departure from your previous company/employer was on good terms.

If the hiring manager was impressed with your CV and you were able to leave a great first impression, he'll be secretly hoping that you were not the problem. However, he'll want to have an idea as to how you conducted yourself during the departure. This means you'll have to provide some indication that you handled your departure professionally. How do you do this? By offering references.

Never say anything negative about your former company/employer/colleagues. Don't mention the involvement of other people in your departure. Moreover, refrain from giving more than one reason for leaving your previous job.

Take a look at this example:

"Actually, I've been seeking an opportunity to demonstrate and develop my skills. I'm not certain I would've been able to do this at my previous position. I left on good terms but right now, I'm here because I am certain that I possess the necessary skills to further my career at your institution."

This is a great answer and no one would even suspect that the speaker left a previous employer on bad terms. It's not as though he/she has told a blatant lie. The speaker merely chose to provide an ambiguous, yet smart, response which focuses on the future.

5) What was the most difficult situation that you've encountered and how did you handle it?

Read between the lines. What the interviewer actually wants to know is this: *"If you were already working for me, will you crack under pressure and take the whole team down with you?"*

Understand that your interviewer is trying to determine your critical thinking and problem-solving skills.

This is the kind of question which calls for one of your on-the-job "war stories." Although you may have encountered and sailed through a bunch of challenging situations, pick the one that is most closely related to the job position that you're applying for. Ask yourself: *What are the problems that I am most likely to encounter in this line of work?* Then determine how you can tie that up with your past experience.

In answering this type of question, concentrate on highlighting your transferrable skills rather than your technical skills. The best skills you can emphasize are your creativity, resourcefulness, and perseverance.

6) What are your greatest strengths?/What are your greatest weaknesses?

When answering questions about your strengths, the trick is to fit them with the requirements of the position and the unspoken needs of your employer. Ask yourself: *Which of my traits will make my potential employer look good? Which of my skills will make his job easier for him?*

As for weaknesses, don't go so far as denying that you have any. Instead, mention your strengths first and mention lots of them. After that, state only one weakness. Choose the weakness which has the *least* to do with your target job position. For instance, you can admit that you're not very good with numbers if the job you're applying for doesn't really require you to deal with numbers on a regular basis. Don't elaborate on your weakness. Keep it brief and straight to the point. Never mention how this will potentially affect your work performance.

Another trick is to mention a weakness that is actually a "strength in disguise".

Example:

"Perhaps my greatest weakness is that I would sometimes grow impatient with coworkers concerning delays in their part of the task. It's just that missing deadlines bother me a lot."

After this, say no more as though indicating that you're prepared to move on to the next question.

7) What is your most notable accomplishment?

Whatever accomplishment that you choose to mention should be in line with the target position that you're applying for. You may have a long list of accomplishment and some of them may seem smaller than others. That said, don't measure your accomplishments according to *your* standards.

Instead, measure them according to the company's needs.

For instance, you may think that the fact that you managed to get a small business mentioned in a popular journal may seem like a humble feat compared to when you prevented a company from accruing thousands of dollars in debt. Even so, if the greatest concern of the company you're applying for is how to gain public exposure, then mentioning the first accomplishment would benefit you more than mentioning the second one.

While talking about your accomplishment, convey genuine passion and pride through your voice and body language.

8) What are your future goals?

The reason why interviewers ask this question is because they want to know if you intend to stick around or if you're just trying the position on for size until something better comes along. A high employee turnover rate is costly for a company. This increases expenses associated with hiring and training.

Regardless of the truth, your answer should focus on the target job position and the company's wellbeing.

Example:

"I intend to grow with a well-established company. I believe that a company like this will provide me with an opportunity for continuous career growth and will enable me to assume more responsibilities in the future as I continue to contribute to the organization's success."

9) How do you handle competition?

What your interviewer actually wants to know is that you have a positive attitude when it comes to competition. Employers are looking for employees who are up to besting the business competition. Thus, your answer should reveal that you embrace competition not only because you like winning but also because you recognize its positive effects on the business/organization.

Example:

"I would describe myself as a competitive worker. I believe that some competition can be healthy in the

workplace as it brings out the best in everyone. Ultimately, competition can benefit the organization as a whole."

10)   How much should we pay you?

This question is like the blade of a guillotine hanging over your head all throughout the interview. It's a question you're afraid to ask but would really, really want to know the answer to. It's a question that your interviewer will inevitably bring up although deep down, you wish he wouldn't. That's because both the interviewer and the applicant are aware that whoever brings up the figure first places himself at a vulnerable position for negotiating. Nevertheless, your interviewer might try to sneak the question in through an inquiry similar to this: *"How much are you making in your current job?"*

What do you tell him then?

Ask yourself these two questions:

- How much are you worth?

- What is your practical range?

Prior to showing up at the interview, make it a point to research your *market value*. That is, the going rate for a professional with your experience and skills. You can search for the figures online or look it up in professional journals related to your field.

The *practical range* refers to the minimum amount that you need to support your lifestyle.

To arrive at a range that you won't be sorry for, bracket the income range so that it slightly goes above the upper range of your market value. It must also be higher than your practical range.

Example:

If, according to your research, your market value is $76,000 - $83,000, and based on your calculations, your practical range is about $77,000, then tell the interviewer that your salary range is: $79,000 – $86,000.

Important: In general, you must avoid the topic of salary until you have been completely informed about the scope of the job and until the interviewer has gained a complete understanding of your qualifications. Delay salary talk until you reach the final interview and until you're certain that you've convinced the employer that his company needs you.

The Post-Interview Phase

So the interview is over. What should I do next?

Don't spend the post-interview phase waiting for the phone to ring. Instead, use it for drafting a professional thank you letter to your would-be employer. Apart from being a traditional act of courtesy, a thank you letter will ensure that your application becomes more prominent in your employer's mind. If you were unable to close the sale with your closing statement during the interview, this is the opportunity to do it.

A thank you letter is a business letter and not a note or a postcard. It should be printed or emailed. It should contain about four paragraphs.

Start off by thanking the interviewer and stating how pleased you were to meet him. Next, express your excitement over the possibility of working in his company. Include a summary of the highlights of the interview. Remind the interviewer of your selling points. Finally, in the closing statement, restate your understanding of when you expect to obtain a response from the employer.

If you were interviewed by more than one interviewer, make sure that each of them receives a different version of the letter.

View a sample of an effective thank you letter on the next page.

Mary Stuart

1234 Lakewood Ave.

Chicago, Illinois 60640

Telephone: 000-000-0000

Fax: 000-000-0000

Email: marystuart@gmail.com

Mr. Paul Smith

Chief Nurse

Mercy Hospital and Medical Center

2525 S Michigan Avenue

Chicago, Illinois, 60616

Dear Mr. Smith,

Thank you for the opportunity to interview for the position of staff nurse. The vitality and intelligence of everyone I spoke with at your offices left a strong impression on me. I am extremely grateful for the warmth and sincerity by which my application was received. I am also thankful for the interest shown in me.

I am thrilled at the prospect of working at Mercy Hospital and Medical Center. You have established a solid team, which I would like so much to be a part of.

I was very pleased with our conversation and especially excited about the idea of the _____ project, which I believe will positively transform patient care. As mentioned, I played a significant role in planning and implementing the _____ Project in _____ Hospital, which led to ____ % less incidences of falls and fall-related injuries in patients within one year. I learned a great deal from that experience and I wish to apply all that I've learned at Mercy Hospital and Medical Center.

Thank you very much again for the stimulating and productive interview. I look forward to hearing from you, as agreed upon, within the next two months.

Sincerely,

Mary Stuart

Final Thoughts

An interview can be a daunting idea for most applicants. But that's only because most applicants believe that they don't have control of the situation. However, as you've learned from this book, an interview enables you to take charge of how you would present yourself to the interviewer. How the interviewer will see you is entirely up to you. The *you* that the interviewer will be meeting with on that day will be the version of yourself which you decide to show him. So, on that day, be the *very best* version of yourself.

When the anxiety begins to creep in, cling to the comforting thought that even if the interviewer is the one asking the questions, that doesn't mean that he has to be the one leading the conversation. The ball is in your court. Play well.

Most importantly, remember to play the role of the salesman and to outwardly focus on the employer's needs while inwardly focusing on your own needs. Keep in mind that in the interview room, no one else will work to make you look good except for yourself.

Lastly, when you do get that job that you've always dreamed of, strive to be the person that you portrayed on that interview. Continue being the best professional version of yourself and you'll be amazed at how far it will take you.

Good luck with your endeavors,

David Barron

References

Dodaj, A. (2012). Social Desirability and Self-Reports: Testing a Content and Response-Style Model of Socially Desirable Responding. Europe's Journal of Psychology.

Retrieved from: http://ejop.psychopen.eu/article/view/462

Frieder, R. E., et al. (2015). How Quickly Do Interviewers Reach Decisions: An Examination of Interviewers' Decision-making Time Across Applicants. Journal of Occupational and Organizational Psychology.

Retrieved from: http://onlinelibrary.wiley.com/doi/10.1111/joop.1211 8/full

Sackett, P. R, Walmsley, P. T. (2014). Which Personality Attributes Are Most Important in the Workplace. Perspectives on Psychological Science.

Retrieved from: http://pps.sagepub.com/content/9/5/538.short

Smith-Genthôs, K. R., et al. (2015). The Tongue-tied Chameleon: The Role of Non-conscious Mimicry in the Behavioral Confirmation Process. Journal of Experimental Social Psychology.

Retrieved from:
https://www.researchgate.net/publication/2676287
06_The_tongue-
tied_chameleon_The_role_of_nonconscious_mimicr
y_in_the_behavioral_confirmation_process

Shroeder, J., Epley, N. (2015). The Sound of Intellect:
Speech Reveals a Thoughtful Mind, Increasing a Job
Candidate's Appeal. The Journal of Psychological
Science.

Retrieved from:
http://faculty.haas.berkeley.edu/jschroeder/Publicat
ions/Schroeder&Epley2015.pdf

About the Author

David Barron is a performance coach and management consultant from Vancouver, Canada. Through his work, David aims to guide individuals and executives in reaching their personal and professional goals. His personal mission is to live his life better than he did yesterday, and his goal is to make that mission a reality for every other person that he comes in contact with.